CHAMPION MUTHLE

SHAKE THE CART!

The Art of Creative Disruption and Millennial-Driven Innovation

Shake The Cart!

The Art of Creative Disruption
And
Millennial-Driven Innovation

By

Champion Muthle

DEDICATION

For my friend Nick.

The Original Cart Shaker who died in action.

A true Gentleman and a Scholar.

May you rest in peace.

INTRODUCTION

Once upon a time in Rio, my friends, Nick, Brett, Sam and me were taking in our first Carnival. It was our first group vacation since meeting each other in Cannes, France a year earlier while working in the Advertising Industry. There we were, just a bunch of Mad Men.

Before meeting up with our friend, Bruno, a Rio local, we decided to hit Copacabana Beach, which was conveniently located just in front of our hotel.

We arrived just in time for a massive beach party. The sand was packed with festival-goers of all shapes and sizes. The music was incredible and the vibe was unlike any other.

There was only one problem. About halfway through the party, the speakers (perfectly positioned in shopping carts spread throughout the beach) blew out.

It was like we were in a movie. Everyone stopped and looked at each other in confusion.

"What do we do now," they wondered?

I'll never forget what happened next.

Just as the panic was about to reach its peak, one person had the balls, brains and...balls to walk over to the speakers and *shake the cart*. That person was my good friend, Nick Huppert.

All of the sudden, boom! The music was back on! The crowd went wild. It was as if our team had just scored the winning goal at the World Cup.

Even I stood wide-jawed in amazement at what had just occurred. Panic turned to pure joy and everyone felt it. Nick became a legend that night...a goddamn legend, I tell you!

The next morning I asked Nick what magic he had used to bring the music back?

He grinned and laughed: "Buddy, I just shook the cart," he said.

"...Just shook the cart," I mumbled dumbly...

"Incredible!"

That's been our motto ever since: Shake the cart!

Like traveling salesmen, we espoused our philosophy everywhere we went.

It became our go-to inside joke.

Late for work? Shake the cart!

Out of gas? Shake the cart!

At the bar feeling shy? Better shake that cart!

Everywhere we went, in everything we did, we. just. shook. the. cart.

I even used it in client pitches...

"What your brand needs to do is 'Shake the cart!'"

Although somewhat comical, the phrase encapsulates, for me, the spirit of bravery, creativity, and innovation we so desperately need in today's world and workplace.

If Nike has "Just Do It," we have, "Shake The Cart!"

It's in this spirit that this book was born.

And it's in this spirit that Millennials should approach work, as bringers of disruption and innovation.

And so, in honor of Nick's triumph that night, I give you **Shake The Cart!**

Cheers,

Champion Muthle

Hakalau, Hawaii

May 18th, 2020

CHAPTER 1

SHAKE THE CART!

I wrote this book for two reasons:

1. Everyone else seems to have a clever marketing book with a catchy title, so I thought I should have one too. JK.
2. To firmly establish the voice of Millennials in the workplace: A generational battleground soon to be liberated!

Don't worry, this isn't another one of those self-help books. It's more of a protest piece.

A lot has changed since the old days, but somehow the workplace has remained stagnant.

The old 9-5 is no longer 9-5, and the office is no longer an office.

But it sure still seems that way. It's time for change.

Millennials already know this of course.

But what about HR?

What about your parents?

Do they even know what that fancy new job title means? Or what it is, exactly, that you do?

Probably not.

That's a problem.

It's a problem because it undercuts your value.

It also downplays your contribution to the economy and undermines your authority in the workplace.

Let's imagine, if you will, that one day a genius disruptive thinker came along and devised a strategy for [The Four Hour Work Week](), or a book for Managers called [The One Minute Manager]().

Now imagine that the world continued working the same way: 9am-5pm. Endless meetings. Zero results.

Madness! Complete madness, I say!

Who's to blame for such stupidity?

It goes without saying, of course, that this has already happened.

The world is still doing the 9-5 thing, 7 days a week, 365 days a year.

And HR is, well, still HR.

Hence my dear friend Tim Ferriss' foray into psychedelics.

(I feel your pain, Tim. Kindly pass the psychedelics).

Oy! Snap out of it!

The point of this book is to shake us from our stupor and remind us that Creative Disruption and Millennial-Driven Innovation are essential.

At the very least, they can save us a whole lot of time. Time that might be better spent doing psychedelics. :)

When I started my first job, I had no idea what to expect. 10 years later, I'm thankful just to have made it out of the office alive.

The critical lessons I've learned along the way, I present to you in this fun little book.

My hope is that you, the next generation, will not only survive the office, but THRIVE.

Alas, I say again, go forth and SHAKE THE CART!

CHAPTER 2

THE VILLAIN: HR

There's a favored story among philosophers about Ludwig Wittgenstein and Bertrand Russell.

Before transforming the world of Academic Philosophy with the introduction of the concept of Language Games, Wittgenstein was a Graduate student at Cambridge under Bertrand Russell.

Having already written the bulk of *Tractatus Logico-Philosophicus,* Russell invited Wittgenstein to present it as his doctoral thesis.

As legend has it, upon presenting his thesis, Wittgenstein remarked to both Russell and G.E. Moore, "Don't worry. I know you'll never understand it." To that, Moore replied in his report, "I consider that this is a work of genius but, even if it is not, it is well above the standard required for a PhD degree." And with that, Wittgenstein passed his defense with flying colors.

Russell and Moore did indeed struggle to understand some of the ideas introduced by Wittgenstein, but they didn't let that stop their young colleague. Thanks to their wisdom, Wittgenstein would go on to write the *Blue* and *Brown Books*, which might never have been published had Russell and Moore rejected his thesis at the outset.

Hence the principle of Philosophical Charity. Now imagine that Russell and Moore are HR and Wittgenstein is a Millennial.

Instead of rejecting Wittgenstein's thesis, certainly the easier thing to do, Russell and Moore had the wisdom and charity to admit what they didn't understand and accept its value and brilliance nonetheless. This is the essential ingredient missing in the modern workplace.

It is with the same wisdom and philosophical charity that HR should approach their work. Otherwise they should cease to exist altogether. Indeed, they're power is already in steady decline. You get the point.

I can't tell you how many times I've encountered prehistoric HR people stuck in the ridiculous patterns and practices of the past. It's not worth retelling here except to say that their behaviour mirrors that of a disgruntled nightclub bouncer or jilted ex-girlfriend. Fear seems to be the overriding factor.

When we fail to understand something we often reject it out of fear, ego or laziness. In so doing, we miss out on the very thing that could help our businesses thrive.

The same is true in the workplace. When HR allows their egos to take over they often end up killing good ideas before they can take shape. This often occurs out of simple ignorance of the larger idea or a failure to see the bigger picture. What a waste!

Ironically, this trend towards risk aversion is actually one of the biggest risks a company can take.

The cost of missing the value of a good idea can be far greater than the cost of implementing the idea itself.

More importantly, a good idea can come from anyone and anywhere: an intern, a competitor, a janitor, a valet. Hell, even HR.

We often become complacent or rigid in the face of an idea or goal that doesn't seem readily ascertainable or valuable. But this is, in fact, where some of the most innovative ideas come from. To ignore or reject them is to ignore or reject your own destiny.

Luckily, there is an antidote for this kind of behaviour: Strategic Bravery.

CHAPTER 3

THE HERO: STRATEGIC BRAVERY

In his long lost 1926 *Letter to the Comintern*, Italian Philosopher Antonin Gramsci demonstrated perhaps the best act of valor and bravery of any technocrat in history.

As Stalin and Trotsky battled for control of the Communist Party, many comrades looked upon the feud in dismay, though none dared protest for fear of incurring Stalin's wrath.

Although the Great Purges were still ten years away and Trotsky's assassination even further off, Stalin's cut-throat tactics were already well known by then.

Stalin's consolidation of party power was a forgone conclusion and most in the party knew it. Only one man, other than Trotsky, was brave enough to stand up to Stalin publicly. That man was Antonin Gramsci.

The strategy Gramsci employed was a surprising but effective one.

In a brilliant Letter to the Comintern, Gramsci first attacked Stalin's nemesis, Trotsky, which gave him the coverage he needed to then counter with an even more devastating criticism of Stalin, Gramsci's true target.

In this way, Gramsci captured the attention of both parties without raising the suspicion of either. One would be hard pressed to find another example in history where someone criticized Stalin publicly and lived to tell about it.

Like a good parent, Gramsci found a way to discipline two feuding children equally and openly. In so doing, Gramsci demonstrated the key characteristics lacking in today's business leaders: Strategic Bravery.

When no one else dared to speak out against Stalin, Gramsci found a way to do it with the stroke of a pen. With his letter, Gramsci demonstrates the power of what I call the *Disruption Mindset*. We'll explore this in the next chapter. Suffice to say that when we open ourselves up to the Disruption Mindset all roadblock are eliminated and anything becomes possible. Courage is contagious. Thus, the Disruption Mindset empowers others to be more effective and creative leaders, as well.

CREATIVE DISRUPTION CASE STUDY #1
OFFICE HOURS

Creative Disruption can be quite a simple process. You just observe, see what's missing, and then do something creative to solve the problem. As a VP in the Communications Industry, I was delighted to have been given my own office. I relished the opportunity to build a friendly workspace. But I quickly realized it was having the opposite effect. For months I watched a steady flow of people walk past my office. Instead of bolstering collaboration, the office was putting a distance between me and my colleagues. That's when I had the idea to create *Office Hours*. Like a college professor, during two four-hour periods throughout the week, I invited my colleagues to swing by my office and chat, have a drink, put their feet up, and take a break. We could talk about anything. Preferably not work. Hell, we didn't even have to talk, we could just sit there and relax. It was an immediate success. After months of not meeting anyone, I suddenly met the entire office within the span of a few weeks. Even the janitors. It was truly amazing and rewarding for everyone, and a definite benefit to the company. It's the little things like this that can make a big difference to the culture of a company. People are people, not robots. Creative Disruption should create an opportunity to enhance our collective humanity and human spirit, not reduce it. When we give our colleagues opportunities to engage and interact in informal settings and nontraditional ways the entire world benefits.

CHAPTER 4

THE JOURNEY: THE DISRUPTION MINDSET

As we've seen, the office can be an extension of the Academic realm and the Political realm.

Like Russell and Moore in the Academic realm, the *Disruption Mindset* requires that we let go of our fears and ego so that true transformation can take shape. To do so requires courage, bravery, and strategy like Gramsci in the Political realm.

What must not be overlooked, however, is the essential element of creativity. We'll look at Creativity in the next chapter. First, it's important for us to define what we mean by "Disruption" and the "Disruption Mindset."

There is a surprising lack of literature on disruptive innovation. Most of the available writing focuses on academic or traditional definitions of the term. This is mostly from the point of view of how companies can avoid being disrupted, or how they can identify opportunities for disruption.

The focus of this book, however, is on developing what I call the *Disruption Mindset:* A mental model for life and business that opens doors to new possibilities for innovation rather than closing them.

This may seem like an obvious notion, but the Disruption Mindset is actually quite a rare gem.

The office has traditionally been a cruel place, filled with society's worst biases and hierarchies. It is, for the most part, the psychological wasteland of our time, where insecurities, egos and Machiavellian machinations run rampant. It is under these unfortunate conditions that disruption has become the outlier, not the norm. Believe it or not, your paycheck is actually hush money meant to keep you in indentured servitude until you finally keel over and die.

Most people go through their lives living to work as opposed to working to live. In fact, perhaps the biggest difference between Millennials and Gen-X is that Millennials *work to live* whereas Gen-Xers *live to work*. It seems to be hard-coded into our DNA.

When we step into the workplace we're actually entering a thoroughly controlled environment that is traditionally filled with the mental models and biases of the generations before us (emphasis on before us, not above us).

For example, while 93 percent of executives say they know their industry will be disrupted at some point in the next five years, only 20 percent feel they're highly prepared to address it. This is because they've failed to master the *Disruption Mindset*.

Thus, it is up to Millennials to be the drivers of creative disruption, or suffer the consequences of convention and cultural stagnation.

CREATIVE DISRUPTION CASE STUDY #2

THE INVISIBLE BRIEF

If you've ever worked in Marketing or Advertising then you're familiar with a client or creative brief. "The Brief," as it's called, is an almost godlike document with the supposed power to make or break a creative project or client engagement. To Traditionalists (or sycophants, as I call them), the brief is irreplaceable, immutable, and untouchable. Without a well written brief, they say, all is lost! The very idea of doing work without one would be considered sacrilege, unbecoming, and unprofessional. The problem is that most creative briefs are either horribly conceived, horribly written, or both. Among seasoned Strategists and Creative veterans, however, there is an unspoken understanding that at the end of the day, there really isn't a need for a creative brief if you're good at your job and know what the hell you're doing. It's almost always the unseasoned and insecure people (who don't know what they're doing) that demand a brief. That's because they literally wouldn't know what to do without it. The deeper problem is that even a well written brief has the tendency to limit creativity rather than expand it. Sure, there's some value in a well focused brief, but not at the expense of creativity itself. This is why as the Director of Strategy & Innovation at a global media agency in New York, I gave my team the opportunity to try something new. I called it *the Invisible Brief.* It's still there, it's just invisible. The Invisible Brief is a decentralized, nontraditional process of developing creative ideas without the need for a physical creative document or centralized development structure. It is an opportunity for teams to improvise, innovate, and intuit free from the restrictions of the workplace. We used the Invisible Brief for 1 out of every 3 client pitches. The results were amazing! Instead of a creative brief, we'd hold standing meetings in the lobby of our building (the old

Carat office near the Empire State building) and gauge the reaction of visitors to certain ideas and creative assets. As soon as something clicked, a pair of strategists and creatives would run upstairs and start developing the idea. What was once a boring, week-long process, became a highly entertaining and stimulating hour long exercise in free association. Voila! Even the Traditionalists were satisfied. The brief was there, it was just invisible.

CHAPTER 5

CALL TO ACTION: MILLENNIAL-DRIVEN INNOVATION

Products with innovative functions assist people in their daily lives and keep society moving forward. They also bring joy to people and inspire new cultures.

As Seth Godin writes in *Crossing the Chasm*, "The safety zone has moved. Conformity no longer leads to comfort. But the good news is that creativity is scarce and more valuable than ever. So is choosing to do something unpredictable and brave."

Millennials are often criticized for being lazy, overindulgent, and impatient simply because we work *differently*. Whereas other generations attach a negative value judgement to the word *different*, Millennials embrace it as their raison d'etre.

In the age of commoditization and industrialization, it is quite possible that this *difference* is the last bastion of originality and truth.

Indeed, Millennials are "good" at Creative Disruption because of the very fact that we value originality and authenticity. We are naturally different and proud of it. We also happen to be the most highly educated generation in the world.

Millennials have learned to distill the lessons of the past into our daily lives. In so doing, we innately give ourselves permission to think outside the box and start fresh, to reset and reboot, and to break from the tyrannous trends and traditions of the past.

In the words of an old Chinese proverb, "To be for one day entirely at leisure is to be for one day an immortal." Thus, to be at leisure at the office is a particular kind of courage that is essential for creative disruption and innovation to take shape.

The Disruption Mindset is a leap into the unknown; it requires a degree of courage for which there is no immediate precedent or reward. Thus, Creative

Disruption and Millennial-Driven Innovation go hand-in-hand.

CREATIVE DISRUPTION CASE STUDY #3
INTERN MEET CEO

I'm always amazed by the power of a simple introduction. Often, a simple introduction is all that's needed to launch someone's career, make everyone a shitload of money, or change the world. And yet it rarely ever occurs. People are so overprotective of their networks and contacts. The key to innovation is unlocking these resources and putting them to good use. As an award-winning Writer and Creative Strategist, I always laugh when people fail to see the value in certain projects or investments. It's just an indication of their own shortsightedness, group thinking, and insecurities. That's why as a young Strategist at McCann Worldgroup in New York, I made a point to introduce our CEO to the brightest and most promising young interns at the company. The results were incredible. Not only did the interns benefit tremendously, but both the CEO and me walked away having gained deep and valuable insights into the culture and lifeblood of the company, insights that we couldn't have gained any other way. We launched several successful projects as a result of those encounters and the interns went on to do great things. I'm honored to know that we've had a lasting impact on the culture of such a storied institution as McCann. It's pretty obvious that every company and CEO in the world would benefit from meeting their interns (and paying them well).

CHAPTER 6
TENSION: CULTURE SHIFT

In a brilliant [blog post](#) about Creative Disruption, the Crypto Venture Capital firm, [Electric Capital](#), describes the process by which Disruption occurs: "A form of disruptive innovation occurs when a cultural shift is combined with utilitarian technology that allows the culture shift to scale."

They point to blockchain technology and the collapse in traditional trust structures as the perfect example of disruptive innovation.

Pointing to the rise of Uber and the 'Sharing Economy,' Electric Capital notes, "When disruptive innovation rooted in a behavior shift occurs, it happens dramatically and the markets it creates are much larger than anyone expects." This is how a $10 billion-dollar taxi market became a $1 trillion-dollar rideshare market, and a multibillion-dollar payday for Uber.

As the firm points out, "When (1) people shift their behavior (often in ways that seem silly at first) in pursuit of utility and (2) technology enables these new behaviors at scale, dramatically improved solutions can emerge." The resulting equation looks something like this:

Behavior Shift + Software = Step Function Change

It is this "Step Function Change" that leads to Culture Shift. For example, as EC describes:

"A decade before Uber, you could hail a random stranger on the streets of Moscow and negotiate a cash payment for them to drive you somewhere. Mobile phones and GPS enabled ride sharing at scale, but ride sharing also required people to shift their behavior and be comfortable getting in a stranger's car. People did this because it was ultimately a step function improvement over calling a taxi. As both software and culture came together, a $100 billion+ industry emerged. These evolutions are not easy in the short term as they may displace existing companies and may have unexpected second order effects. In the long term, however, innovations drive dramatic improvements in efficiency, productivity, and quality of life. Mobile phones disrupted PCs, which disrupted mainframes, which disrupted the slide rule."

As EC and others conclude, "We should embrace disruptive innovation for its long-term benefits while being mindful of its near-term consequences."

Put simply, innovators and intrapreneurs can help champion disruptive innovation by working to identify the emergent human behaviors and opportunities that exist down the line. Because these behaviours may seem silly at first, the opportunity to outmaneuver the competition and benefit from these changes is immense. Change agents can bolster their position by identifying these opportunities early, building buy-in, and engaging stakeholders in a way that allows companies to take advantage of the Step Function Changes of the future.

CREATIVE DISRUPTION CASE STUDY #4
NAP TIME

Never underestimate the importance of sleep. My 6th grade Social Studies teacher Mrs. Baker was always adamant about nap time. I loved her class. I always left feeling rested, rejuvenated, and full of inspiration. Now that I think about it, it was my favorite class. Indeed, I probably went on to love and study history as a result of that feeling that nap time gave me. Math on the other hand was another story. Ironically, my Canadian math teacher was always angry and impatient. The exact opposite of Mrs. Baker. He could've probably used more sleep. Now, as an adult, I'm a big believer in having nap time at work. The benefits could be endless. We would feel more rested and perform better. We would slow down and allow ourselves to breathe a little. There would be opportunities for collective dreaming and subconscious collaboration. And, perhaps most importantly, we'd leave the office feeling a bit better about our companies and more inspired to return to work the next day.

Namaste. :)

CHAPTER 7

CLIMAX: THE SHAKY-CART CURVE

When we look at the industries and areas with the highest potential for disruptive innovation, the true value of adopting a Disruption Mindset becomes clear.

Biggest Opportunities for Disruptive Innovation

IDEA	VALUE	SCOPE
Digital Transformation	$100 Trillion	Global
Asteroid Mining	$100 Trillion	Global
Open borders	$78 Trillion	Global
Disruptive Technologies	$14 - $33 Trillion	Global

E-Commerce	$22 Trillion	Developing Countries
Wealth Management	$22 Trillion	Global
Smart City Tech	$20 Trillion	Global
Artificial Intelligence	$15.7 Trillion	Global
Climate Change Mitigation	$7 Trillion	Global
Advancing Women's Equality	$12 Trillion	Global
Free Trade	$11 Trillion	Global
Circular Economy	$4.5 Trillion	Global

Closing Gender Pay Gap	$2 Trillion	OECD
Longer Working Lives	$2 Trillion	OECD
Empower Young Workforce	$1.2 Trillion	OECD
Car Sharing	$1 Trillion	Global

Only a handful of people would have guessed the sheer dollar size of the Disruption Market: $431.4 *Trillion*. And almost nobody would have guessed that Asteroid Mining would be at the top of the list. As the rate of technological change and population density increases, so too will the multiplicative value of the Disruption Market. Thus, Disruptive Innovation is not just hype or a fancy catchphrase, but a tremendously valuable Corporate Asset and a unique business opportunity.

But the true value of Creative Disruption can only be computed once we consider the real rate of technology adoption. To do so requires taking a look at three fundamental formulations: The Technology Adoption Lifecycle (or Roger's Bell Curve), the Technology Hype Cycle (Gartner), and the Kübler-Ross Change Curve. When we bring the three together, we get what I call *The New Adoption Curve* or *Shaky-Cart Curve*.

The Technology Hype Cycle

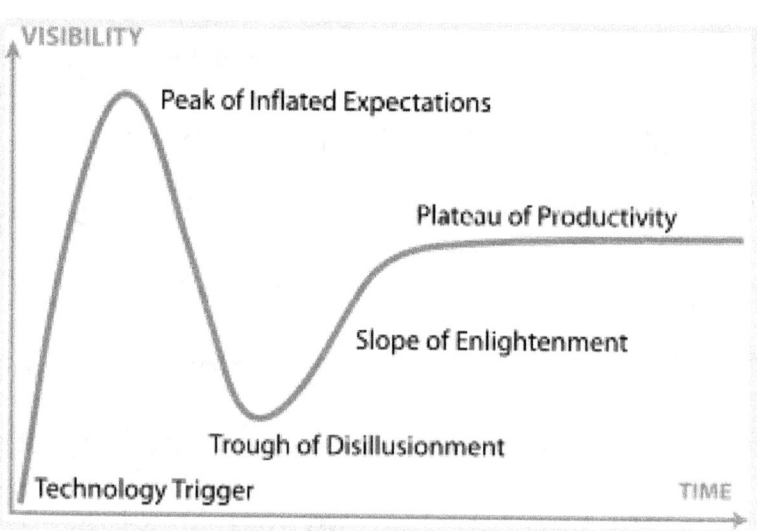

Roger's Bell Curve

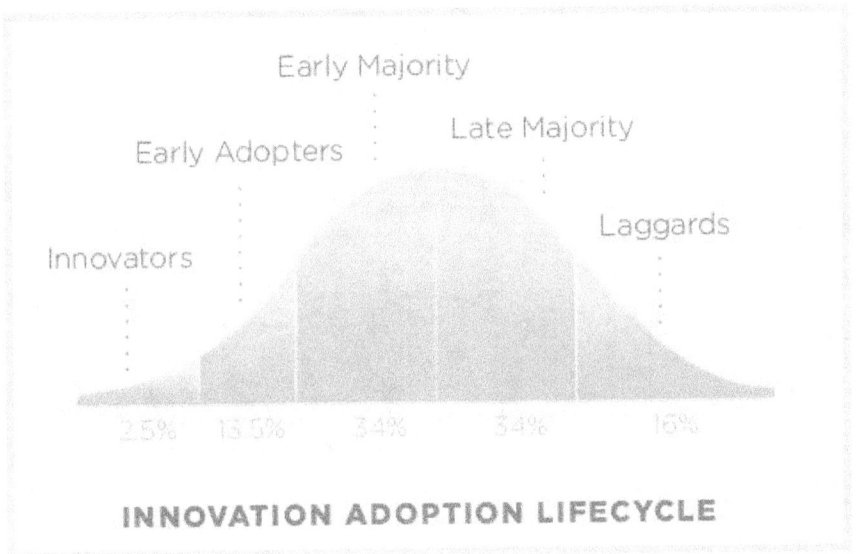

Kübler-Ross Change Curve

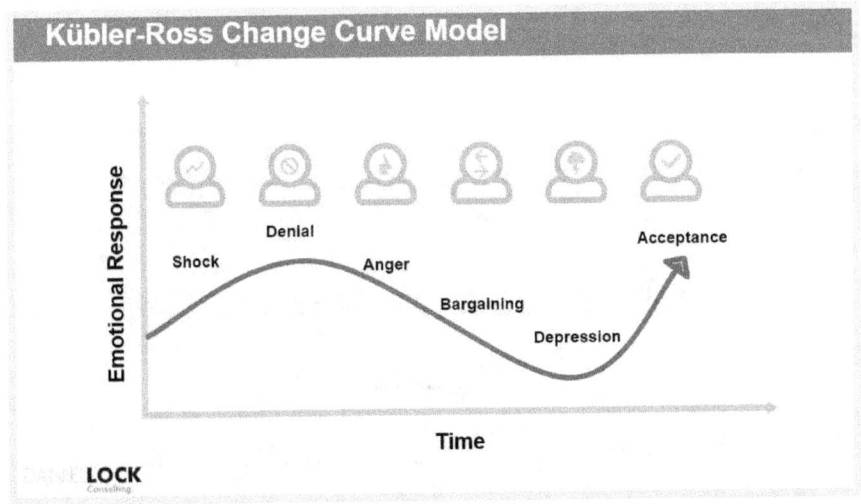

The New Adoption Curve

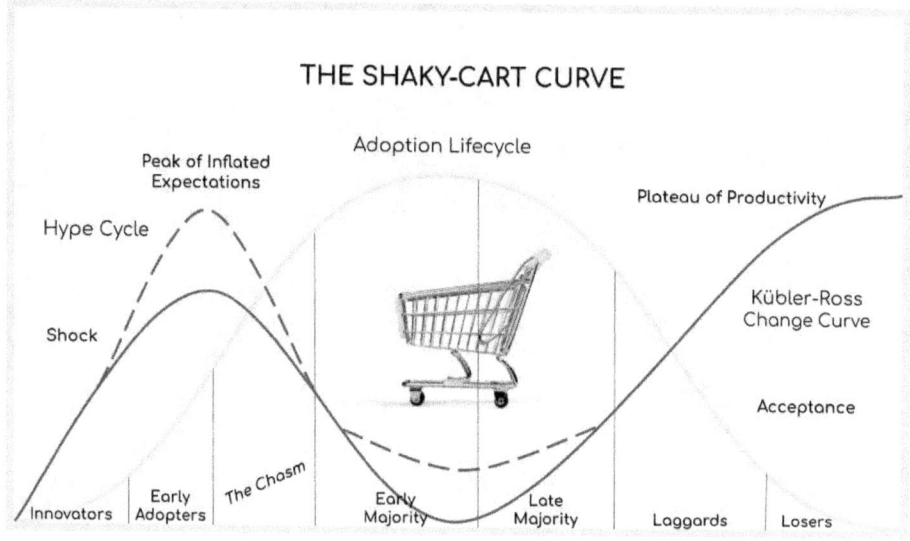

The New Adoption Curve is our guiding light through a sea of technological darkness. It is our roadmap, nay, treasure map, to the lucky charms of true disruptive innovation!

CREATIVE DISRUPTION CASE STUDY #5
FAIL CAMP

Failure is an inevitable part of life. It shows up everywhere, even at work. Indeed, the thought of workplace failure is probably one of the biggest, if not the biggest, causes of stress in our adult lives. Which is why it's so important to embrace failure at the office. During my time as a Digital Strategist at the World Bank, that's exactly what we did. As a member of the World Bank Innovation Team, we organized Fail Camp, a recurring series of meetups and happy hours during which time we would share our worst workplace failures from the previous few weeks. As the resident Social Media Guru, my talks usually focused on my latest efforts to get a group of high-level World Bank Economists to start blogging and tweeting. But when it did come to more serious failures, I was very happy to have someone with whom to share my stories. Needless to say, Fail Camp was a huge success with one of highest event turnouts at the Bank. Everyone saw the value of sharing their failures; participation never dwindled. I'm sure if we did a study it would show that performance and morale improved significantly as a result of Fail Camp. I certainly had a good time.

CHAPTER 8

RESOLUTION: THE WAY OF THE CART

I used to joke with my colleagues that our goal should be to innovate ourselves out of a job. As intrapreneurs, I argued, we should be pushing our bosses to innovate so hard that they either give in to our demands or get rid of us.

"If we're not being threatened with layoffs every other quarter then we're doing something wrong," I joked.

In hindsight, I might have lost a few jobs for it. Bummer, yes. Worth it, probably not. But the idea stands. Innovation is bigger than all of us, and certainly any one of us.

In his groundbreaking book, **The Talent Mandate**, executive Andrew Benett highlights the importance of developing a diverse and dynamic talent pool while creating an innovation-centered workplace.

In addition to building appreciation for the difference that Millennials bring to the table and promoting an entrepreneurial spirit in the workplace, Benett also aptly emphasizes the need for open debate and flattened decision making.

"The companies pushing the talent revolution forward," he writes, "have at least three qualities in common:

- They embrace a diversity of ideas.
- They encourage debate.
- They accept failure."

I couldn't agree more. In fact, I believe these three qualities form the basis of an entirely new way to work, and are critical elements of what I call *The Way of The Cart*.

Like the **Tao of Work**, or the **Ambidextrous Organization**, *The Way of the Cart* represents the resolution of our journey through Creative Disruption and Millennial-Driven Innovation. It can be expressed in twelve simple steps that every company, entrepreneur, and business leader should follow:

The Way of the Cart

1. Get Rid of HR, Focus on Talent
2. Put People First, Including Customers
3. Be Brave, Be Creative
4. Adopt a Disruption Mindset
5. Champion Millennial-Driven Innovation
6. Embrace Culture Shift
7. Follow The New Adoption Curve
8. Trust Your Talent and Treat Them Right
9. Be Different, Be Original, Be Authentic
10. Be Relentlessly Adaptive
11. Drive Endless Innovation For All
12. Define Your Higher Purpose

CREATIVE DISRUPTION CASE STUDY #6
ZEN VENTURES

Today there is perhaps no other industry more ripe for disruption than Private Equity and Venture Capital. Sadly, Silicon Valley, once the nexus of innovation and entrepreneurship, has become the citadel of inequality, discrimination, and disenfranchisement. I encountered this first-hand as a seasoned entrepreneur living in San Francisco from 2019-2020. It was one of the worst experiences of discrimination, injustice, and inequality of my entire life. As a Civil Rights leader, that's saying a lot. Indeed, I found Silicon Valley to be the very heart of inequality and economic disparity in America, with Los Angeles not far behind. You wouldn't expect it with all those bubble jackets and new Teslas (which makes it all the more frightening to think about). Black founders receive less than 1 percent of venture capital. 81 percent of VC firms don't have a single black investor, and only 2 percent of VC partners are black. This is a glaring injustice, one that must be confronted on a national scale. This is why I decided to create [Zen Ventures](), an impact venture studio for diverse founders. At a time when black founders are being actively blocked from funding and investment, our goal is to increase financial inclusion, enrich the growing community around diverse founders, and deepen global investment in the technology, tools and infrastructure that will allow our generation and the next to thrive, create, and grow. I believe it is the perfect example of how Creative Disruption and Millennial-Driven Innovation can transform an entire industry. After all, Venture Capital is no longer about deciding if a startup will be a success or failure, it's about understanding where startups exist on the New Adoption Curve. Zen Ventures is the first diversity firm to use a startup studio model at its core. Whereas other funds raise outside capital to invest in outside startups, Zen Ventures builds, grows and funds our startups internally to maximize the value of our technological and financial impact on society and the markets. To date, over a dozen traditional VCs have pledged to focus funding towards Black founders and startups, but this is just the tip of the iceberg. There's a lot more work to be done. In order to see real change, Venture Capital will have to invest heavily in innovative firms like Zen Ventures that are championing Creative Disruption and Millennial-Driven Innovation across the globe.

www.ingramcontent.com/pod-product-compliance
Lightning Source LLC
Chambersburg PA
CBHW070839220526
45466CB00002B/831